GROWING YOUR DIGITAL BUSINESS

EXPANDING YOUR SOCIAL WEB

COLIN WILKINSON

ROSEN
PUBLISHING®

New York

To my family, for motivating me to continue to build on everything that is great in my life, and my wife, Ami, for continuing to show me how great it is to be motivated

Published in 2013 by The Rosen Publishing Group, Inc.
29 East 21st Street, New York, NY 10010

First Edition

Library of Congress Cataloging-in-Publication Data

Wilkinson, Colin, 1977–
Growing your digital business : expanding your social web / Colin Wilkinson.—1st ed.
    p. cm.—(Entrepreneurship in the age of apps, the Web, and mobile devices)
Includes bibliographical references and index.
ISBN 978-1-4488-6929-9 (library binding)—
    ISBN 978-1-4488-6974-9 (pbk.)—
    ISBN 978-1-4488-6975-6 (6-pack)
1. Electronic commerce. I. Title.
HF5548.32.W535 2013
658.8'72--dc23

658.8
Wilkinson

2012006968

Manufactured in the United States of America

CPSIA Compliance Information: Batch #S12YA: For further information, contact Rosen Publishing, New York, New York, at 1-800-237-9932.

CONTENTS

INTROD

When running a business, a digital entrepreneur can reduce risks—and maximize success—by planning beyond the initial product launch. The expansion of a product through content updates, new features, and improvements has become an expectation of most users. Maintaining communication with customers helps today's entrepreneurs build a better product and continue to improve it over time. By making use of existing—and often free—technologies, today's developers also have the potential to quickly reach expanded markets and identify new customers.

With expanding markets come a growing customer base and many accompanying responsibilities. With the high levels of competition online, digital

entrepreneurs must invest in their customers in order to succeed. Properly engaging the customer base with content updates and interaction helps keep them returning to your mobile app, Web site, blog, or game. With returning customers, entrepreneurs see a return on their investment through sales, word-of-mouth advertising, and valuable usage data.

Monitoring the growing business using financial tools and sales reports provides digital developers with the information needed to properly plan for further expansion, whether that means moving to larger offices, hiring new teams, or building more products. Understanding the financial side of doing business is an important skill to have for all entrepreneurs. With some practice, it provides not only a proper snapshot

Team planning is an ongoing process that helps to define and develop your business.

of the company's revenue and progress but also leads to planning for additional success. Every business has the potential for growth, but maintaining success while balancing the burdens of a growing business requires diligence, motivation, and proper planning.

CHAPTER 1

THE FINANCES OF DOING BUSINESS

Understanding the basics of business finances can be easier than one might think. It is an essential part of creating a success out of any business plan. Of course, a key aspect of evaluating a business's finances is measuring revenue—the total amount of money coming in from sales and other sources.

However, an even better measure is to look at a business's income, sometimes called net income. This is the total revenue minus any and all expenses. Net income defines how much money a business actually makes after taxes and other expenses, such as costs for Web hosting, employee payroll, or reference materials. Income and expenses are typically calculated over a set amount of time. For example, you might list your annual income or your monthly expenses.

In short, revenue includes all money coming in, expenses include all money going out, and income is the difference between the two. In fact, it's possible to have a negative income, which would mean that the business was not profitable during that period of time.

BOOKKEEPING

A key job in every digital business, outside of designing a product, coding a feature, or even communicating with customers, is the task of managing the books. Bookkeeping means managing the financial records of the business. The work includes accurately recording revenue and expenses, as well as planning for future business investments. It's important to record all financial transactions with enough detail that

Tracking expenses is more than just a tedious chore. These valuable records lead to better spending and smarter decision making as the developing business grows.

someone else can interpret them, even several years down the road. Without these records, it can be impossible to determine how successful the business is and how much it has grown. Accurate records will also be needed come tax time. Down the road they may become invaluable when looking for a business loan or attracting investors.

Digital businesses, especially when starting out, often have a relatively small set of expenses. Without employees to pay or monthly rent on an office space to manage, one might wonder why it is still important to maintain accurate records. A digital business may be a one-person operation and not even intended to be a primary source of income. Does it matter how successful the business is? Absolutely! Reporting accurate earnings and expenses at tax time is something all businesses are legally required to do. Solid bookkeeping can also be the key to planning the future of one's business, including identifying opportunities for growth.

FINANCIAL PLANNING DAY-TO-DAY

Developing and maintaining a budget is not always an easy task. When it competes with decidedly more exciting and creative aspects of a business, finding time for proper accounting may be difficult. The best rule is to set aside some time each day. It doesn't need to be much: often just fifteen minutes will be enough to record any expenses and revenue and to do a quick status check to see how everything is doing.

Setting aside time to regularly review business revenue helps to identify any upcoming needs and verify the business's momentum. An accountant or financial adviser can help guide you.

Tracking cash flow is, in essence, no different than balancing a checkbook. Expenses and revenue are listed as positives and negatives. They are added together to determine the total amount of money available to be used for future investments, expenditures, or simply set aside for a rainy day.

Another financial chore that should become a regular item on any business's to-do list is reading any bills or receipts that come in for accuracy. Financial fraud has become a big problem, and it can be easy to miss an incorrect credit card charge with only a glance at the bill. Make sure that all expenses listed are valid, and if something seems incorrect, take action immediately. Taking on the responsibility for a business's finances includes the job of ensuring they are correct and safe.

When planning for a purchase, it's important to be sure the timing is right. An entrepreneur needs to answer some important questions. What is the value of the purchase? How will it help the business? Is the purchase going to increase profit and, if so, how long will it be before that occurs? Will the purchase pay for itself in the long run? These are all key questions that need satisfactory answers when making a purchase for the business. Thinking carefully about these questions will help weed out the "wants" from the "needs." Sometimes less expensive alternatives, or better timing for purchases, can be identified with simple planning.

A tricky expense to calculate, especially for many businesses just starting out, is the cost of research and development. It's easy to overlook the time you spend learning a new technology or reading about how to create a business plan. A task can be valuable even if it isn't directly tied to the product. Proper research can prevent hassles later on and can eventually increase the success of a business. Additionally, many states provide tax breaks for young, small businesses that invest in research. When you record research expenses, include instructional manuals,

SUCCESSFUL TOOLS FOR MANAGING FINANCES

The following are some electronic tools that can help you track and manage finances for your digital business:

- **Quicken**. This personal finance software helps with money management and expense tracking.

- **Intuit QuickBooks**. This business accounting software helps with expense tracking and payroll.

- **PayPal.** You can set up a merchant account and track incoming payments using this company's payment solutions.

- **Mint.** This site allows you to track spending trends across multiple bank accounts.

- **Wesabe.** This site offers online money management with the support of a social network, allowing users to provide and receive financial advice from its online community.

books, and courses you take. You should also include the cost of developing a core technology. This is a key component of the product that has the potential to be reused outside of the product. For instance, time spent developing an infrastructure for accepting purchases, while it may be used for the business's initial product, can also be used in all future products. Therefore, it could potentially fall under the research and development umbrella. It can be helpful to consult with an accountant when recording research and development expenses. He or she can answer your questions and help you resolve anything you are not sure about.

BANKING AND FINANCIAL TOOLS

As your business grows, so will its financial needs, and a trusted bank can help you manage growth and profit. Finding the right bank may require some leg-work. There are a number of online tools for identifying banks and credit unions that support small businesses. Also, speaking with other local businesses or mentors can be a great way to find a positive banking experience.

Speak with your bank's representatives about your goals for your business. Bank representatives are often able to provide some support and steering as you are getting up and running, based on their experiences with similar endeavors.

Another important destination is the local county clerk's office, where you can file the paperwork to initiate your business. While there, you can also gain a wealth of information about local organizations dedicated to helping small businesses succeed. Once your business has its own checking account, a paper trail is generated for all transactions that go through that account. This eases the task of bookkeeping and adds security to the business's finances.

In today's digital world, many tools have been developed for increasing the efficiency of bookkeeping. In fact, many business bank accounts include software to help manage the financial side of a growing business. It is still important to review information for accuracy and ensure that no important expenses are missed.

When looking for software tools to aid in bookkeeping, think about how well the software integrates with your business's other existing tools. For example, if your business accepts payments through PayPal, being able to import a spreadsheet of PayPal history into the bookkeeping software—and to work with the data recorded within the spreadsheet—can be a real time-saver. Deciding which bookkeeping software is right for your business, and when the right time to invest in such software might be, is a great discussion to have with your bank, accountant, or financial mentor.

RAISING REVENUE

For many digital businesses, accepting direct payments is the primary form of revenue. These can include payments for downloadable content, membership fees, or online donations. There are a number of options for accepting online payments that make the process fairly straightforward. For example, services such as PayPal have become an expected way to pay for purchases, and creating an account is a simple process. These services include tools for creating

Using a ready-made payment processing solution, such as PayPal, allows you to accept credit card payments securely. Also, it often provides access to support options and a community of users.

interactive elements, such as online "shopping carts." Better yet, systems like PayPal automatically create their own bookkeeping records and can be linked to a bank account for quick transfers of earnings.

When developing apps for mobile devices, there are specific processes that must be used for transactions. Both Apple's and Android's app stores include an application programming interface (API) for setting up and handling in-app purchases. Other online venues use a similar approach with proprietary payment systems, such as Facebook Credits. Using these established payment methods keeps users in a familiar and trusted environment when making purchases.

Digital businesses also bring in nonpayment forms of revenue by supporting their products with ads. Money comes in when users view or click ads displayed on the screen near your business's main content. This advertising is paid for on a regular basis and can prove very profitable when there is a high volume of visitors.

Whatever your method for raising revenue, it is always a good idea to streamline the process. This may mean providing quick access to in-app purchases with occasional user prompts for purchase. Or, it may mean developing a menu flow that provides single-click access to the store. A tactic that has worked well for a number of apps, including the popular Facebook game Sims Social, is to encourage in-app purchases with regular discounts on items.

The same strategy can be applied to a number of product types. For instance, membership-based sites, such as Netflix, often use discounts to add to their member base by offering a lower cost for the first year of service or providing a free first month of service. Anything you can do to hook users and feed them into the stream of revenue for your business will pay off in the long run.

CHAPTER 2

GROWING YOUR BUSINESS, INSIDE AND OUT

Growing pains eventually become a challenge for any successful business, but with preparation it's possible to forecast what growth means for your business and build a successful plan for expansion. Growth may mean different things for different businesses—bringing on new team members, moving to a new office, or even making the decision to develop and support additional products.

Growth can be a positive experience, as it opens doors, presenting the opportunity to try new ideas that were previously out of reach. On the other hand, growth means added responsibility, whether it be to a broader customer base needing support, a pool of employees expecting to be paid, or a public expecting a new product that is not only as successful, but more successful, than the last one—all without breaking the bank.

In all industries, there are stories of failed businesses that grew too quickly and then couldn't meet the added demands. The digital market is no exception. In fact, in the early 2000s

Growing businesses may require a larger team to successfully take on expanding needs. For example, engineers and technicians can help manage added computing power and storage.

the booming Web industry led to a number of dot-com businesses that grew too quickly. One of the most well-documented examples is Webvan, an online grocery delivery service that failed after expanding into cities across the United States. Deciding when to grow, and managing that growth throughout the process, is key to maintaining your business's success and focus.

EXPANDING YOUR TEAM

For many small businesses, the decision to hire additional workers can be a difficult one. Often the personal qualities most useful in creating a start-up and building an initial successful product need to be balanced by different personalities in order to sustain the company. Identifying the new roles needed in the business is one of the first steps to growing. As a digital business owner, you should look for the developing needs that the company must meet, especially those that require talents or expertise not currently available. Then prioritize what is most essential in carrying the company forward.

One option is to work with contractors, people who are hired to do a specific job within a limited period of time, rather than permanent employees. This can often be a lower-cost and more timely way of meeting an immediate need, such as creating new art or implementing software features. In addition, hiring a worker on a contractual basis allows the entrepreneur a chance to review someone's personality, work ethic, and development process.

Doing this may also give you the time to better define future roles in the company. When making the jump to work with a larger group of people, defining a shared vision for the company and its products can be helpful. You may want to write a mission statement, a short written statement of your business's objectives and its reason for existing. This can give everyone shared goals to work toward and judge output against. Posting these goals where everyone can see them, such as on the front page of the company Web site or on the wall of the office, can help inspire the team to develop the company and its products.

THE DIGITAL INDUSTRY: TYPICAL ROLES

When expanding your workforce, it can be useful to look at typical roles in a similar business and identify which needs are being met and which are not. As a company grows, expectations for its products may increase. Users will look for updated features and content. Developers will want to ensure the product shines and remains competitive. New features often come with additional technology requirements, leading to a need for new skills at the company. In some cases, the current developers can expand their skill set and take on the new requirements. However, often the types of duties that need to be performed make some additional hands on deck the best option.

A common discipline for the digital industry—whether your business creates games, apps, Web sites, or something else entirely—is the engineer. Software engineers are typically responsible for designing the software infrastructures and writing the code. Similar roles that may need filling within a growing company include software testers, technical support, and engineers with a particular specialty, such as networking, databases, or server administration.

An expanding digital business may also need artists and animators to create new content, develop the look and feel of software or Web sites, and develop advertisements or other marketing content for the company. As a product becomes successful and continues to evolve, designers may be needed to create Web site layouts, improve the user experience, make content, or script game-play scenarios.

Outside of development, expanding companies often have a growing need for managers to oversee the additional production and larger teams. They may also need dedicated groups that focus on

Artists and designers often plan the presentation—the look and feel—of a game or other product through a series of concepts and mock-ups.

marketing, customer service and support, or finances. Early on, a single person, or a single team of people, may handle many of these roles, often while also participating in the company's engineering, design, and art efforts. However, after a while, a company can reach a size at which additional management is needed. At this point, team management and team processes become important considerations for the leader of the business.

FINANCING YOUR COMPANY'S GROWTH

As a company grows, its operating expenses increase as well. Additional costs for payroll, computer or software needs, rent and utilities, and customer support all add up quickly. If they are not managed, these expenses could bring an early demise to a budding success.

Financing growth often means looking for outside investment, from a loan or from venture capital. Venture capitalists, who tend to focus on young, tech-focused businesses, can be a great source of financing when looking to grow. However, in return, the investors will be looking to make money on the deal. This adds risk if a company does not turn a profit in the coming years.

When trying to secure funding, lenders will look at the business's revenue to date, any outstanding debt, the business plan, and the state of the business's industry. This last item is especially important: investors

ETSY.COM:
A DIGITAL SUCCESS STORY

Etsy.com is a Web site where people can buy hand-made and vintage items directly from artists and small, independent sellers around the world. In a relatively short period of time, the Web site became a huge success in digital commerce.

- In 2005, a team of four built Etsy's Web site in only two months, based on an initial design by Rob Kalin, then twenty-five years old.
- By the end of 2007, Etsy had seen more than two million sales through its service.
- Building on initial investments, Etsy received an additional $27 million in early 2008.
- In early 2010, Etsy opened a satellite office in Berlin, Germany.
- Today, Etsy operates in multiple locations. It had an expected $72 million revenue for 2011.
- The Etsy for iPhone app, launched in November 2011, reached one million down-loads in less than four months.

will be less likely to provide money to a venture that has little chance of succeeding or one that faces too much competition to stand out. For example, the Web site Pets.com, which aimed to sell pet supplies to customers

Employees at Etsy eat lunch together in the company's New York offices. Digital commerce sites such as Etsy.com rely on strong customer support and a quality user experience to be successful.

on the Internet, went out of business in just nine months after securing $50 million in funding when it could not create enough return from sales.

A GROWING MARKET: BUILDING YOUR CUSTOMER BASE

Once a product becomes successful, bringing it to new markets, and new customers, is a natural expansion. This may mean selling your product in new locations or to new groups of consumers, or creating variations on the original product.

After an app is released or a Web site goes live, additional maintenance, support, and content updates are often required during its life cycle. As your product continues to evolve, it is good practice to watch for opportunities to bring it to new markets. For instance, many mobile apps are eventually released into other countries with translated text. Similarly, as a blog becomes popular, it may incorporate additional topics, broadening its overall appeal.

Reaching more customers means more opportunities to make a sale, more income from ad views, and more potential for increased word-of-mouth advertising and brand recognition.

Building a customer base can take time and can be a bit of a balancing act. For instance, updating an app with new features can keep the interest of users and encourage them to return to the app. However, updates that occur too frequently can confuse users with too many changes or burden them with frequent downloads.

It is also important to make your product easy for new customers to find. This may include updating keywords to keep your product at the top of search results or adjusting the product description so that it appears in the proper categories. You also want to make sure your product's name is different enough from the competition—and simple enough—that a

SALES OF VIRTUAL GOODS: SIMS SOCIAL

In just a few short months Sims Social became the second most popular game on Facebook, allowing players to customize and maintain a digital home, interact with friends on the social network, and complete story missions to earn in-game currency. This free-to-play game became a major factor in its publisher's earnings for the year using in-game purchases driven by real money. The game saw success by encouraging microtransaction sales, or the purchase of virtual, nonphysical goods for use in the game, from its users. The game offers many limited-edition items that appear in its store, regular sales on specific items, and the ability to take shortcuts in the game using in-game currency available for purchase. According to an article in the *New York Times*, the game's power as a business also comes from the fact that players must continually increase their circle of friends in order to advance.

potential customer doesn't have to guess when typing it into a search field.

Attracting new customers has become easier in recent years with the growth of social networks. Making use of social networking tools to provide announcements and advertisements, and funnel users to your

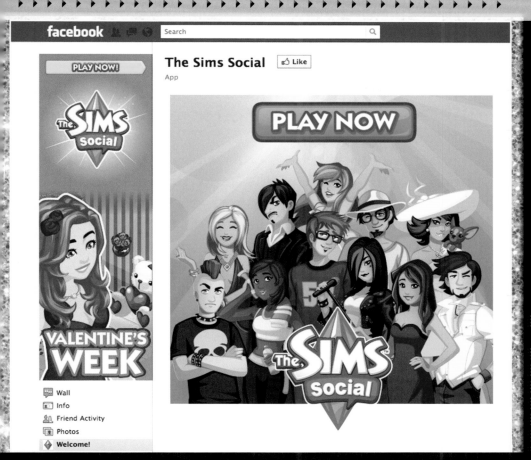

The official Facebook page of The Sims Social (https://www.facebook.com/TheSimsSocial) shows how digital games can succeed by integrating into social networks.

product, can be free and can have a larger impact than more traditional forms of promotion. Some businesses provide discounts via social networking sites in the form of bonus content downloads or price reductions for "liking" their Facebook page or following their Twitter feed. The viral nature of these networks provides a real advantage by linking networks of people together. An entrepreneur can quickly reach an entire group of people with a shared interest and then a series of secondary groups that watch their updates.

Proper use of discounts and sales can help provide a boom in your customer base. When the product includes ongoing revenue support, such as from ads, subscriptions, or additional in-app purchases, a lowered initial price can lead to more customers and higher profits in the long run. Also, having more users leads to more word-of-mouth advertising, which in turn leads to more users.

Many mobile apps with in-app purchases (such as games in which one can pay for additional levels or virtual goods) include occasional short-term sales on additional content. Some offer limited-edition content available for only a short time. As well as encouraging purchases, this strategy provides the bonus of encouraging users to return to the app frequently. Even Facebook provides occasional discounts on its internal currency system, Facebook Credits, used within games and applications. This leads to additional purchasing of the currency, increased time spent on the site, and more user investment in the applications in which they spend the currency.

CUSTOMER COMMUNICATION

One of the most essential elements of bringing in new customers is the proper treatment of current customers. Reading customer feedback and addressing it does not go unnoticed. When customers feel special, they'll not only continue to use the product but will also tell their friends about it and take the time to write a favorable review.

Providing the users with a voice in the product's direction and updates can even reduce risk in your design efforts with what is essentially a dedicated group of free testers. A flaw in the product discovered by an existing user could have become a barrier keeping other potential customers away.

Good communication with customers becomes even more essential as the customer base grows. Upsetting half of your customers when there are only ten may not seem like a big deal, but angering half of several thousand customers can lead to major setbacks or even a company's failure. For example, in mid-2011 a series of poorly planned communications led to the confusion of many Netflix subscribers, with an estimated eight hundred thousand customers canceling the video rental service.

CHAPTER 3

HOW YOUR CUSTOMERS CAN WORK FOR YOU

Customers are the most important component of any successful business. Without the customer there is no audience, no market, and no path to revenue. In addition, your product's users can be an immensely valuable source of feedback, critique, and even marketing. As a digital business becomes more successful, its customer base often grows more than any other resource on hand.

When trying to identify how your customers can help you build a better product, it's important to define what you hope to achieve and what you need to know to reach your goals. For example, a developer with a previously released app might be looking for direction on an update that is under development. Someone with a yet-to-be-released blog might be curious about the average speed of a typical user's Internet connection. Whatever your purpose, you should define some clear goals that can be achieved using feedback and information from and about the users.

USER FEEDBACK

Working with feedback can be full of ups and downs, but it can also be one of the easiest and most successful methods for gathering user data. Some venues, such as Apple's App Store, provide quick methods for users to rate or write a review on the products featured there. While this information may be aimed primarily at other would-be customers curious about a product, keeping an eye on your product's reviews can help you improve the product for users. Checking in about once a week does not require a large time commitment and is typically enough to identify any trends in the feedback users are posting. Many users who feel strongly about a mobile app, game, or Web service will want to share their opinion, whether it's good or bad. It's essential not to let a few negative remarks hurt the team's morale but to use them as an opportunity to build an even better product.

If you plan to work with user feedback, providing a quick and direct method for users to provide it will help encourage a broad set of responses. For instance, mobile apps including Flower Garden have taken to adding in-app prompts asking the user to rate or review the product. When providing a prompt such as this, developers suggest integrating it into the app in a way that doesn't disrupt the user experience or overprompt the user. The easier it is to provide a rating or review, the more ratings will come in.

METRICS

While feedback provides users' opinions on their experience within the product, metrics provide hard data on how users are actually using the product. Metrics come in many forms, including Weblogs detailing how many times a site has been visited each day or which pages are viewed the most. For a game, you might gather data on how many times a player fails within a game's level.

The power of user metrics is in their unbiased nature. For instance, a user may write a review stating that a certain feature advertised within the product doesn't work. However, metrics may show that the feature is buried too deep within the app and users simply aren't finding it—a very different problem requiring a different solution.

When considering implementing a metrics-gathering system, the first step is to identify what information would be most useful. Identifying what engages your users, and what doesn't, can help inform future investment in updates and content creation. Finding points of frustration or confusion can be used to streamline the user experience. Ready-made tools, such as Flurry or Google Analytics, provide easy-to-implement solutions that can be added to existing products to provide immediate access to a wealth of information.

ORGANIZING THE FEEDBACK AND DATA

A large amount of feedback can be daunting to keep organized. Using tools to organize the feedback is an essential step in making sure it is addressed. Organization can be as simple as a whiteboard or corkboard containing all of the tasks that need to be addressed or as complex as a deep bug-tracking software suite with detailed steps to reproduce and fix each issue.

AMS Account Management System   Welcome, GG   Wed Feb 1

« Back to Account Detail Page

2008-2011 Detail Report

Showing usage data for account: Gramercy Games

Export Report »

Filter Dates   From Date: 01-01-201 To Date: 2-15-2012

ip_address	total_duration	total_sessions	avg_duration	total_requests	t
192.168.252.286	0:05:11	1	0:05:11	2	1
192.168.317.67	0:00:18	2	0:00:09	4	2
192.168.204.420	0:09:20	3	0:03:07	25	1
192.168.343.64	0:00:22	2	0:00:11	3	0
192.168.165.212	0:08:39	1	0:08:39	6	0
192.168.275.339	0:20:35	2	0:10:18	14	0

Many digital distribution channels include reports analyzing users' activity. The metrics in these reports provide useful information for developers.

In the end, a team should choose the technique that best fits the scale of their product. Losing time digging through overly complex solutions, or fighting with an inadequate solution, will only stifle the product's development. Tools that are quick to learn and that scale easily for different needs often prove to be the best solution. Online solutions such as UserVoice handle the task of organizing end user feedback and suggestions and can be integrated into your Web site or Facebook page. Other options, such as Trello,

HANDLING CUSTOMER DATA

Businesses are responsible for the content they release to their customers. Digital entrepreneurs often face the additional responsibilities of properly handling their customer's personal data. Keeping sensitive data, from credit card numbers to user names, safe and secure is a necessity in the digital age.

In addition, misuse of a product, such as customers using a product to engage in cyberbullying or hate speech, is a serious aspect of digital ethics and another area of responsibility for businesses. Responsible digital businesses take steps to limit and stop abuse and help educate their users.

focus more on task creation and tracking by using an online digital task board. In fact, Trello uses its own software to track development of new features, bug fixes, and improvements, creating a public list that any user can access and contribute to.

Once the feedback, usage data, and ratings have been gathered, the next step is to prioritize what to address while maintaining momentum on your business's other endeavors. Determining which feedback to address when, and how, can be tricky. Here's a

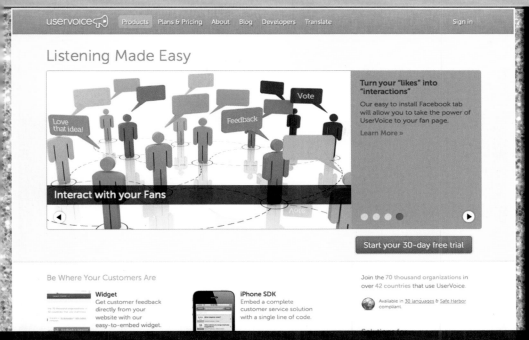

Tools such as UserVoice simplify the process of collecting and managing user feedback and tracking and responding to customer issues.

way to simplify your decision making. Starting with the most requested changes, assign a value denoting the impact of each change (that is, how important it will be to the success of the product) and a value denoting how difficult the change will be to implement. This approach often identifies a few items that can be completed quickly and have a large impact on the user base. These should become high priority changes, while the others will need more consideration. For items that rank high on the

POWER OF THE NETWORK

Social networks have created a wealth of user-driven content and interaction, supporting marketing and sales in ways that were previously unavailable to businesses.

- Gifting items between users, such as in Farmville, encourages users to invite their friends into the game.

- Reposting or "liking" stories shared by friends allows information to quickly travel among large networks of users.

- The use of tagging allows quick dynamic links to similar content or content created by a specific app.

- Simple interactive polls and contests encourage users to become engaged by subscribing to a product's page updates.

- User-provided data advertisements displayed on pages can be catered to individual users or groups of users.

difficulty scale, consider alternate work-arounds that could address, or even remove, the problem with a lower risk and development time.

SHARING IS CARING

Providing users with easy outlets to help market your product can be a "win" for both parties: it can earn you more customers, and it can provide a fun and creative social feature for users. One of the simplest options is a "tell a friend" feature, which allows users to send a precomposed e-mail with a link to the product or specific content within it. In this form of informal advertising, the recipient receives the information from a known, and presumably trusted, source, adding a personal element. Similar to this feature, many Web sites and blogs include a quick link to share or "like" a post, immediately relaying the post to the reader's social network.

Mobile apps and games have caught on to this and now often include options to share game–play milestones and in-app creations on social networks. Gaming networks, such as Steam or Apple's Game Center, allow their users to track their friends' gaming habits, invite each other to multiplayer gaming sessions, and even gift their favorite titles to

The Facebook "Like" button has become one of the Web's most enjoyable and accessible methods for quickly sharing articles, Web sites, and nearly everything the Web has to offer.

one another. Some apps have been able to use sharing features as viral marketing tools, leading to greater numbers of downloads. For instance, the music creation app Beatwave allows its users to e-mail their creations to others in an editable format but requires that the recipients also have the software installed. This is made easy by the download link embedded within the e-mail. Similarly, many successful subscription-based services, especially online games, have introduced ambassador programs that earn bonuses and discounts for their users when they invite their friends to join.

Empowering users with the ability to share their excitement for your product with others, through e-mailed content, social network integration, or invitations to others to try it, can be one of the most rewarding additions to any digital product.

CHAPTER 4

UPDATES AND IMPROVEMENTS: KEEPING CUSTOMERS ENGAGED

U ser engagement refers to the level of participation and interaction around your product. It includes all the ways customers engage with the product, the business, and each other. In essence, it defines when, why, and how users are consuming your Web site, app, game, or blog.

Creating successful forms of user engagement means sustaining users' attention while using the product and motivating the same users to return to the product in the future. Engagement does not necessarily translate to increased initial downloads, but it may result in subscription renewals, increased in-app purchases, or higher ad revenue. More important, users that are engaged tend to spend more time discussing and sharing the product with others, which translates to a larger customer base.

PRODUCT UPDATES

When making updates to an existing product, you'll want to make sure your new and improved content works to reengage users. When a product becomes stale, lacking any new content or features, users will move on from it in search of something else. By continuing to provide new content and interactions,

Popular blogs, including Nate Silver's FiveThirtyEight blog, find success by offering frequent updates on content relevant to their readers. The format also allows news stories to be shared very quickly.

you can ensure that your customers will keep returning and will stay engaged.

In some cases, the simple act of providing an update will reengage users. For instance, when users see that an update is available for an app installed on their mobile device, they tend to be curious. Users will likely want to find out what new content might be available, leading them to launch the app at least once more. This, however, only acts as a catalyst for bringing users into the product. In order to keep them there, the new content needs to have depth.

Consider a blog that might be updated once a month. The average user is going to return to that blog only once a month at the most. In order to build engagement, the blog could be updated more frequently, giving readers a reason to return more often. Another option would be to update with deeper content and interaction, such as a poll or contest.

A model of effective updating, the popular mobile game Pocket God has included regular updates nearly every month since its original release in January 2009. These updates have introduced a variety of new content, including hidden mini-games, multiplayer leader boards, game–play interactions, and in-app purchasable visual customizations. Pocket God players are constantly reengaged by their desire to find the new items. User engagement is sustained over time with the promise of new content released regularly.

Planning for an update's content includes watching user feedback and reviews for desired features. It also allows developers an opportunity to add some features that had originally been cut because of time constraints, cost, or risk. The current trend of having a soft release, or a launch in which some product features are planned for future updates, has made it acceptable to add major features and content after the initial launch. Providing a mix of updates, including new features desired by the development team and features requested by users, has a number of benefits. It improves the user experience, shows users that their requests and

Mark Zuckerberg, founder of Facebook, remains highly involved in the planning of the social network's new features. The company has stepped up its efforts to prepare users for updates.

comments have been heard, and provides engaging new content and surprises.

When all else fails, deciding on a theme for each update can not only motivate the team but can also inspire some new features that had not previously been considered. For instance, Angry Birds Seasons was released as an entirely separate app from the original Angry Birds game. The app provides holiday-themed content updates throughout the year as a fun twist on the more typical updates containing new levels for play.

COMMUNICATING ABOUT UPDATES: A LESSON LEARNED

In 2007, Facebook released a new feature known as the "mini-feed," which displayed a live list of changes, posts, and updates from friends. With no real communication about the impending update, which made drastic changes to the familiar page layout, users quickly became confused and then frustrated as they were bombarded by seemingly random updates. Within twenty-four hours of the update's release, more than 750,000 members had joined groups protesting the change. In a hasty response, the development team poorly communicated their commitment to the members, causing the situation to go from bad to worse. The story of the failed feature reached major newspapers within the next few days. In contrast, the new "timeline" feature rolled out to Facebook users in late 2011 was preceded by multiple communications, tutorials, and help videos. Facebook even allowed users to determine when they would make the switch, as well as preview the changes before making them public.

SCHEDULING UPDATES

Properly timing the release of a product update requires diligence in monitoring the product's use, watching user feedback, and managing the content development for the update. While each update will likely help bring in new customers, its primary focus is to reengage the current users, and releasing the update while users are still enjoying the most recent release or update is a necessity.

As with any work tasks, developing a schedule for an update will ensure that it reaches the audience in a timely manner. The schedule can also be a deciding factor in figuring out what to cut when a particular fix or feature is proving more difficult than initially

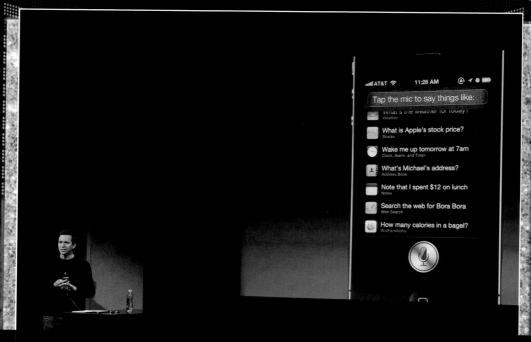

Apple continues to engage its users with frequent updates to its software and hardware, such as the Siri voice-recognition app included within the iPhone 4S.

thought. Creating time estimates for each item included within the update is a solid start. Unexpected items that come up in the middle of development can be weighed against the current and upcoming tasks. If a new item is important, you might be able to swap it for a lower priority item that can be safely saved for the next update. Some updates, such as those for the Apple App Store, require additional time for approvals; this time also needs to be figured into the update's schedule.

Releasing an update is a major investment for any business and should be treated as seriously as an initial product launch. Planning for the update's content is essential, with time dedicated to proper testing and the fixing of any problems prior to launch. Souring a successful product with an update that has not been properly tested has the possibility of alienating customers, turning a success into a fail-ure difficult to recover from, and even marring the brand or business. As with any product launch, it is important to ensure that support personnel are ready to address any customer questions or concerns on the updated content and that any unforeseen issues can be dealt with quickly.

BIGGER, BETTER, FASTER, MORE

Each update brings exciting new content or fixes, all of which take time and resources to develop. It makes sense that this content should help sell the product, and advertising the update is an important aspect of its launch. Your update plan should include updating existing advertising, product information on Facebook, or a product description in the App Store or Android Market. You can also feature a special "New in this version..." banner prominently on your Web site. Highlighting your new content and features, and being responsive to user requests, will help to reengage existing users and attract new users with the knowledge that the product is continually and actively being improved.

Some new features and changes, as vital as they may be, can be too large and create a barrier for returning users. In these cases, providing special assistance with the new features for users migrating from a previous version of the product will help prevent frustration. It will also demonstrate the company's commitment to its customers. For instance, apps like Notes Plus and Flowchart include built-in tutorial screens displaying how to use the app, while the photo-editing app Snapseed includes overlay help tips each time the user accesses a feature for the first time. Other products often include video tutorials or a step-by-step walkthrough for new users. These tutorials illustrate how to get the best experience within the product.

BOOSTING ENGAGEMENT

Increasing engagement from your users is a great way to build success. Providing users with added interaction, however simple, will increase their engagement. When these interactions exist within a social context, the engagement level grows even more. For instance, many businesses have found that posting simple polls or discussions on social networking sites leads to increased visits and more engaged customers. Allowing customers to vote on upcoming features or share their favorite experiences within the product helps build excitement. Providing contests engages users with the promise of a chance to win new content or discounts for "liking" a page, rating an app, or sharing content from within the product. Feeding this energy into ongoing updates can help build momentum and maintain user engagement leading up to the launch.

CHAPTER 5

MOVING INTO NEW MARKETS

Expanding into new markets can be an exciting and promising step forward for any business. It can help to remotivate the development team and add engagement to the customer base. New markets, whether they are new regions for sales, new types of products, or simply a new set of customers, help widen the company's reach and can increase profits.

Bringing an existing product into a new market may involve providing additional product support to address the needs of a new group of users, or it may require translating the content into a foreign language. It may be as involved as designing and developing an entirely new product within the existing brand. Successes in market development include top-selling video games that are released overseas or Web sites that develop spinoff sites using the same approach and technology but with content aimed at a different audience.

EVALUATING NEW MARKETS

When considering the leap into new markets, the company should carefully identify which markets are best suited for the product and have the highest

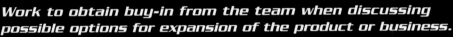

Work to obtain buy-in from the team when discussing possible options for expansion of the product or business.

potential for success. Many times this information can be garnered from the existing audience by reading the feedback and reviews, viewing metrics on who is using the product, and questioning users directly with polls or surveys.

When evaluating a new market, consider what the composition of the audience might be. Look at the size of the potential audience and review the key differences between the current customer base and the new audience. Every difference may impact how the product is viewed. For instance, differences in users' locations could create the impression that a multiuser Web site has a low level of traffic, when in reality the existing customer base is sleeping at the time that its new users are accessing the site. If there is uncertainty, it is worth the time to continue researching the new market, ensuring that the product demand exists. To avoid surprises like this, taking a look at how other similar products have moved into new markets can be a valuable time investment.

Before moving into development, conduct an analysis that weighs the cost of moving into the new market—including the time necessary to implement any needed changes, added marketing and support costs, and any material or hosting costs—against the potential for sales within the new market. In some cases, expanding into new markets may not require much work at all, such as releasing a mobile app into an online store overseas without additional language support. In this way, a company can test the waters of new markets with very little initial investment.

MAKING A PLAN

Developing a market expansion plan is similar to planning an initial product launch or creating a strategy for an update. List all development tasks that need to be completed prior to the launch. Then add launch and post-launch tasks, such as additional support considerations. Creating a timeline for the launch is key, and reaching incremental deadlines along the way will help keep the work focused and in check. Continue to

LOCALIZATION

Localization is the process of translating a product for new regions. It encompasses not only translation of the language, but also changes needed for content that might insult or confuse users in other regions. Localization is an important aspect of bringing products into new regions successfully. While it may be true that English speakers are found the world over, statistics from other countries have shown that proper localization leads to a more successful release. For instance, download statistics of iOS apps in China have shown that apps translated to the local language have more success, with nearly half of the titles in the top twenty-five downloads using localized names. This trend has encouraged companies such as PopCap to ensure that its games receive proper localization to remain successful when arriving in other regions of the world.

monitor the costs and time along the way to gauge the success of the venture and to better plan for further expansion.

Moving into new markets adds responsibility and, if not properly planned for, may spread the company's resources too thin. Beyond the needs of a growing customer base, there may be a language barrier in providing product support or a time zone difference that results in delayed responses.

Market differences may also include technical differences. For instance, when bringing an Android app to the iPhone, there may be different standards requirements, operating systems and memory allowances, and user interface styles. If you are targeting a new set of Web site users, it is possible that they may have slower computers, smaller monitors, no speakers, old browsers, and missing plug-ins. However, when reaching out to these new markets, it is important to provide them with the same quality of user experience, support, and communication that has made the product a success in previous markets. Similarly, new audiences will expect the same commitment to updates and fixes that other users have come to expect.

TESTING

As with all launches, testing is key to a successful release. When changing markets, proper testing can become tricky. Not only might testers need knowledge in a foreign language or a different set of expensive mobile hardware, but they may also need to become familiar with a different set of social norms.

Whenever possible, find users from the new target market who are willing to test the product. This can often be done through contests or notices on the product's Web site. Many game developers provide limited access to "beta" versions of their product—

pre-release software that is still being fine-tuned and prepared for final release—to identify bugs and receive feedback from the intended audience. This can often be much cheaper and more successful than paying for a full testing team. Finding testers within the intended market also helps identify any unforeseen problems, such as differences in how a checkmark on a button may be interpreted in different regions of the world. Similarly, while services like Facebook may be huge in the United States, successfully bringing social games to other parts of the world requires investigating the popular options available there.

BREAKING OUT WITH TRANSMEDIA

Transmedia is a unique form of bringing a product into new markets. It involves the coordinated use of storytelling across different media platforms. With transmedia, users invested in the story of the product, or learning more of the product's fictional universe, follow the product across mediums and markets. For instance, movies are often accompanied by video games that give a different perspective on the story or act as a prequel to the film's story. More recently, many digital companies have begun accompanying their flagship product with comic books that help fill in missing story elements. The popular mobile app Pocket God has done just this with comics, an animated Web series, and a spinoff app. Similarly, the game Angry Birds, which includes almost no narrative, commissioned an animated video to be created that adds to the brand's story. After a year and a half, the video, posted on YouTube, has received more than fifty million views. Since then, the company behind Angry Birds has committed to a project for an animated TV or Web series, with potential for a movie as well.

Another successful transmedia project, Inanimate Alice is a transmedia novel told across multiple platforms. It has been adopted as a learning and reading comprehension tool. The story unfolds through video, audio, text, and interactive game play, and it empowers its readers to help tell the story. Updating the story across multiple episodes, the author and development team leave room for students to create their own episodes, providing a sense of ownership and increasing the readers' investment in the story.

Transmedia can be a profitable approach to marketing a product because it gives customers a greater sense of investment and ownership. Also, by reaching the audience in whatever venue they might be—on their mobile device, on Facebook, in a bookstore, on YouTube, or watching television—they can continue to be close to the product no matter where they are. However, the wealth of content required for a transmedia approach means it takes a good deal of work to get going. For transmedia to work, consistency is key. Story and presentation, including the style of writing and the look of art, should be consistent across all markets. This is essential in maintaining brand recognition, so that the audience will immediately tie the various products together as existing within the same brand universe.

Transmedia, such as the cross-platform narrative Inanimate Alice, allows a product to break the barriers between different mediums.

When making the jump to transmedia, one of the first questions to ask is what platforms provide the most impact, quickly followed by which platforms present the easiest transition. However broad the approach taken, transmedia can be a rewarding investment for the developer as well as the customer.

Building a digital product for continued success can take many directions, including adding new features, markets, content, and forms of media. Whatever your goals, doing proper planning, teamwork, testing, and data analysis is a sure way to get there.

GLOSSARY

ACCOUNTANT A person who is professionally trained in accounting or keeping the financial and tax records of a business or person.

APPLICATION PROGRAMMING INTERFACE (API) Programming code that allows components of the software to communicate.

BUG A software defect.

CASH FLOW The movement of money in and out of a business.

CUSTOMER BASE The customers to whom a business sells products and services and on whom it focuses most of its efforts.

DATABASE Computer data stored in a structured set.

ENGAGEMENT The active interest and action of the customer base with regard to a product or a brand.

EXPENSE Money spent on something in a business's efforts to generate revenue.

IN-APP PURCHASE Purchase of an upgrade, new content, or special features directly within an app.

LOCALIZATION The practice of adjusting the features of a product to fit the language and culture and other differences of a foreign market.

MARKET The selling opportunities provided by a particular group of people.

METRICS Data gathered about a digital product and its users.

GLOSSARY

MICROTRANSACTION A small payment made for virtual goods to be used in a video game, app, or online community.

MISSION STATEMENT The documented values and goals of an organization.

NET INCOME The total revenue in an accounting period, minus all of the expenses during the same period.

R&D Research and development; the process of discovering new knowledge and using that knowledge to develop new products or procedures, or to improve existing ones.

REVENUE The income generated from selling goods or services, before any costs or expenses are subtracted.

TRANSMEDIA Storytelling that occurs over multiple media platforms, often involving active participation by the audience.

VENTURE CAPITALIST A private investor that provides capital (start-up money) to a promising business venture.

AIGA, The Professional Association for Design

164 Fifth Avenue

New York, NY 10010

(212) 807-1990

Web site: http://www.aiga.org

The AIGA is committed to advancing design as a professional
craft, strategic tool, and vital cultural force.

Institute of Electrical and Electronics Engineers (IEEE)

2001 L Street NW, Suite 700

Washington, DC 20036-4910

(202) 785-0017

Web site: http://www.ieee.org

The IEEE is the world's largest professional association dedicated to advancing technological innovation and
excellence for the benefit of humanity.

International Game Developers Association (IGDA)

19 Mantua Road

Mount Royal, NJ 08061

(856) 423-2990

Web site: http://www.igda.org

The IGDA is dedicated to improving developers' careers and lives
through community, professional development, and advocacy.

National Association for the Self-Employed (NASE)

P.O. Box 241

Annapolis Junction, MD 20701-0241

(800) 649-6273

Web site: http://www.nase.org

The NASE was founded in 1981 to provide day-to-day support for the self-employed, including direct access to experts, benefits, and consolidated buying power that traditionally had been available only to large corporations.

National Federation of Independent Business

53 Century Boulevard, Suite 250Nashville, TN 37214

(800) NFIB-NOW (634-2669)

Web site: http://www.nfib.com

The NFIB's mission is to promote and protect the right of members to own, operate, and grow their businesses.

World Organization of Webmasters

P.O. Box 1743

Folsom, CA 95630

(916) 989-2933

Web site: http://webprofessionals.org

The World Organization of Webmasters is a nonprofit professional association dedicated to the support of individuals and organizations that create, manage, or market Web sites.

WEB SITES

Due to the changing nature of Internet links, Rosen Publishing has developed an online list of Web sites related to the subject of this book. This site is updated regularly. Please use this link to access the list:

http://www.rosenlinks.com/deaa/dibi

Chaney, Paul. *The Digital Handshake: Seven Proven Strategies to Grow Your Business Using Social Media*. Hoboken, NJ: Wiley, 2009.

Clark, Josh. *Tapworthy: Designing Great iPhone Apps*. Cambridge, MA: O'Reilly, 2010.

Cockrum, Jim. *Free Marketing: 101 Low and No-Cost Ways to Grow Your Business, Online and Off*. Hoboken, NJ: Wiley, 2011.

Coupey, Eloise. *Digital Business: Concepts and Strategy*. 2nd ed. Upper Saddle River, NJ: Pearson Prentice Hall, 2005.

De Kare-Silver, Michael. *E-shock 2020: How the Digital Technology Revolution Is Changing Business and All Our Lives*. Basingstoke, UK: Palgrave MacMillan, 2011.

Goldman, Jay. *Facebook Cookbook*. Sebastopol, CA: O'Reilly, 2009.

Kerpen, Dave. *Likeable Social Media: How to Delight Your Customers, Create an Irresistible Brand, and Be Generally Amazing on Facebook (& Other Social Networks)*. New York, NY: McGraw-Hill, 2011.

Lesonsky, Rieva. *Start Your Own Business: The Only Startup Book You'll Ever Need*. 5th ed. Irvine, CA: Entrepreneur Media, 2010.

Rowse, Darren, and Chris Garrett. *ProBlogger: Secrets for Blogging Your Way to a Six-Figure Income*. 2nd ed. Hoboken, NJ: Wiley, 2010.

Weber, Larry. *Everywhere: Comprehensive Digital Business Strategy for the Social Media Era*. Hoboken, NJ: Wiley, 2011.

BIBLIOGRAPHY

Bohrer, Isabel Eva. "Social Networking Sites Taking Action." Center for Digital Ethics and Policy, Loyola University Chicago, November 28, 2011. Retrieved December 5, 2011 (http://digitalethics.org/2011/11/28/essay-social-networking-sites-taking-action).

Cotriss, David. "8 Tips and Resources for Managing Your Business Finances." Small Business Trends, September 10, 2009. Retrieved September 24, 2011 (http://smallbiztrends.com/2009/09/tips-resources-managing-business-finances.html).

Edwards, Cliff. "Netflix Declines Most Since 2004 After Losing 800,000 U.S. Subscribers." Bloomberg.com, October 25, 2011. Retrieved November 25, 2011 (http://www.bloomberg.com/news/2011-10-24/netflix-3q-subscriber-losses-worse-than-forecast.html).

Fleming, Laura. "A New Model of Storytelling: Transmedia." Edutopia.org, August 26, 2011. Retrieved September 24, 2011 (http://www.edutopia.org/blog/transmedia-digital-media-storytelling-laura-fleming).

Goltz, Jay. "Avoiding the Growth Trap." *New York Times*, October 13, 2011. Retrieved November 25, 2011 (http://boss.blogs.nytimes.com/2011/10/13/avoiding-the-growth-trap/?scp=8&sq=managing%20small%20business%20finances&st=cse).

Kim, Ryan. "Urtak Unlocks User Engagement and Insights with Collaborative Polls." *New York Times*, May 13, 2011. Retrieved September 30, 2011 (www.nytimes.com/external/gigaom/2011/05/13/13gigaom-urtak-unlocks-user-engagement-and-insights-with-c-12561.html?partner=rss&emc=rss).

Ko, Andrew J., Michael J. Lee, Valentina Ferrari, Steven Ip, and Charlie Tran. "A Case Study of Post-Deployment User Feedback Triage." Information School, University of Washington, 2011. Retrieved September 30, 2011 (http://faculty.washington.edu/ajko/papers/Ko2011UserFeedbackTriage.pdf).

Llopis, Noel. "Increase Your App Ratings on the App Store." Games from Within, June 14, 2010. Retrieved September 24, 2011 (http://gamesfromwithin.com/increase-your-app-ratings-on-the-app-store).

McManus, Brendan. "Facebook Freebies Can Build a Strong Customer Base." VentureBeat.com, March 30, 2010. Retrieved September 24, 2011 (http://venturebeat.com/2010/03/30/how-to-use-facebook-freebies-to-build-a-customer-base).

Millward, Steven. "iOS Download Stats for China Show the Importance of App Localization." Tech in Asia, 2011. Retrieved December 5, 2011 (http://www.penn-olson.com/2011/11/25/ios-china-app-localization).

Spool, Jared M. "Learning from the Facebook Mini-Feed Disaster." User Interface Engineering, July 16, 2007. Retrieved October 20, 2011 (http://www.uie.com/articles/facebook_mini_feed).

Ulken, Eric. "Measuring User Engagement: Lessons from *BusinessWeek*." OJR: The Online Journalism Review, April 16, 2009. Retrieved September 24, 2011 (http://www.ojr.org/ojr/people/eulken/200904/1696).

Weber, Larry. *Sticks & Stones: How Digital Business Reputations Are Created Over Time and Lost in a Click.* Hoboken, NJ: Wiley, 2009.

INDEX

ABOUT THE AUTHOR

Colin Wilkinson is a professional video game developer and has previously operated a successful Web development company and nonprofit community arts organization and gallery. In between shipping games, he operates a small dairy farm with his wife in upstate New York.

PHOTO CREDITS

Cover, p. 1 © istockphoto.com/Ismail Akin Bostanci; pp. 3, 4–5 © istockphoto.com/loops7; p. 6 StockLife/Shutterstock; pp. 7, 17, 30, 39, 48 © istockphoto.com/Dennis Glorie; p. 8 Kurhan/Shutterstock; p. 10 © istockphoto.com/Steve Debenport; p. 15 © istockphoto.com/tomch; p. 18 Comstock/Thinkstock; p. 21 © Tom Koene/ZUMA Press; p. 24 Todd Heisler/The New York Times/Redux; p. 35 © UserVoice; p. 37 © istockphoto.com/pressureUA; p. 40 Beth Rooney/The New York Times/Redux; p. 42 © AP Images; p. 44 Kevork Djansezian/Getty Images; p. 47 Antonio Mo/Taxi/Getty Images; p. 49 Chris Clinton/Digital Vision/Thinkstock; p. 55 © The BradField Company, Ltd. 2005–2011; interior backgrounds image (glitter) © istockphoto.com/Tobias Helbig; interior background image (graphics equalizer) © istockphoto.com/Silense.

Designer: Brian Garvey; Editor: Andrea Sclarow Paskoff; Photo Researcher: Marty Levick